One Forest, Different Trees

by Kim Fields

illustrated by Linda Howard Bittner

Scott Foresman
is an imprint of

PEARSON

Glenview, Illinois • Boston, Massachusetts • Chandler, Arizona
Upper Saddle River, New Jersey

Every effort has been made to secure permission and provide appropriate credit for photographic material. The publisher deeply regrets any omission and pledges to correct errors called to its attention in subsequent editions.

Unless otherwise acknowledged, all photographs are the property of Pearson.

Photo locations denoted as follows: Top (T), Center (C), Bottom (B), Left (L), Right (R), Background (Bkgd)

Illustrations by Linda Howard Bittner

16 ©Mark Wilson/Getty Images

ISBN 13: 978-0-328-51425-0
ISBN 10:   0-328-51425-X

Copyright © by Pearson Education, Inc., or its affiliates. All rights reserved.
Printed in the United States of America. This publication is protected by copyright, and permission should be obtained from the publisher prior to any prohibited reproduction, storage in a retrieval system, or transmission in any form or by any means, electronic, mechanical, photocopying, recording, or likewise. For information regarding permissions, write to Pearson Curriculum Rights & Permissions, One Lake Street, Upper Saddle River, New Jersey 07458.

Pearson® is a trademark, in the U.S. and/or in other countries, of Pearson plc or its affiliates.

Scott Foresman® is a trademark, in the U.S. and/or in other countries, of Pearson Education, Inc., or its affiliates.

3 4 5 6 7 8 9 10 V0N4 13 12 11 10

One day Sue's third grade class decided to make a big picture for the wall. They wanted to make a forest. Each student tried to draw a tree for the forest. But there was a problem—a big problem. "We don't know how to draw trees!" said Amy. All she drew was a wavy green line.

"I can help," Sue said. She loved drawing trees.

"You are the best artist!" Amy said.

"What's *that*?" asked Nat, pointing to Sue's picture.

"That's a tree," said Sue.

Nat shook his head. "Trees look like green lollipops," he said. "What you drew is *not* a tree!"

Sue was very sad. "I worked hard to draw this tree," she said. "These are local trees. They grow all around the state. I make a lot of practice drawings because I want to get it just right!"

"Well, you got it *wrong*," said Nat.

Amy looked at Sue's real-looking tree. Then she looked at Nat's drawing of the green lollipop. "Nat," she asked at last, "will you teach me to draw trees?"

"Sure!" said Nat. He showed Amy how to draw a green circle. "Those are the leaves," he said. Then he drew a brown straight line. "That's the trunk," Nat said.

"Neat!" said Amy. Soon all the other children wanted to draw green lollipops too.

Sue felt sad. She tried to find something nice to say about the other drawings. "Those are nice green lollipops," she said. But no one said anything nice about her drawing.

Nat shook his head at Sue's drawing. "If we're going to have a forest, all the trees should look the same," he said. "Draw green lollipops, Sue."

Sue started to make a lollipop. Then she put her pen down. She couldn't do it.

When the bell rang, everyone ran outside. Sue stayed behind, working on her drawing. She didn't feel like being social. Sue's teacher, Mr. Martinez, saw her sad expression. He always encouraged his students to do their best work. "That is a very good tree!" he said. He gave Sue his support.

"The other kids don't think so," said Sue. "They want me to draw the way they do."

"Do you want to draw lollipop trees?" Mr. Martinez asked. Sue shook her head. "Then don't!" he said.

"Drawing a tree that looks like a lollipop is easier for some people. And sometimes kids want to do what everyone else does. That's social pressure. But that doesn't mean you have to do it," said Mr. Martinez.

"I can draw all sorts of trees," Sue said. "I can draw one that looks like an octopus," she said. "And one that looks like a monkey! I can also draw one that looks like a beautiful, real tree!"

For the rest of recess, Sue drew. She didn't think about what the other kids might say. She thought only of how happy she was to be drawing.

The class came back from recess. "Did you make a tree that looks like a lollipop?" asked Nat. Sue showed them her drawings.

The class saw the tree that looked like a monkey. They saw the tree that looked like an octopus. And they saw the tree that looked just like a tree.

"Wow," said Amy. "These are good!"

Mr. Martinez held up Amy's first drawing, the one that was a wavy line. "This is good too." he said. "There is no one right way to draw. Draw what you feel. Don't draw what everyone else tells you to draw.

"In our state we have all kinds of trees," he went on. "Some are native, and some were planted by the people who settled here."

13

Nat picked up Sue's drawings. "Then our forest picture can have all kinds of trees," he said. "They don't all have to look like lollipops."

Sue picked up Amy's picture with the wavy line. "They don't all have to look like real trees, either," she said.

That afternoon, the class put their drawings on the bulletin board. There were lollipop trees and monkey trees. There was Amy's tree that was one wavy line. And in the very center was one special tree. It was Sue's tree. The one that looked just like a real, native tree.

Freedom of Expression

Freedom of expression means we can express ourselves in many different ways. We have freedom to write books that show how we feel. We can make movies that tell the stories we want to tell. We can create songs and pictures that matter to us. It doesn't matter what others think about what we create. What matters is what we think and how our creations make us feel.